# YOUR HIGHWAY CODE TEST MADE EASY

## Brenda Ralph Lewis

**W. Foulsham & Co. Ltd.**

London ● New York ● Toronto ● Cape Town ● Sydney

*W. Foulsham & Company Limited*
*Yeovil Road, Slough, Berkshire, SL1 4JH*

ISBN 0–572–01390–6

Printed in Great Britain by
St Edmundsbury Press Limited,
Bury St Edmunds, Suffolk.

# Contents

# Introduction

This book is designed to help you acquire a sound
knowledge of the Highway Code in an enjoyable and
straightforward way. The subjects covered in the Code
have been divided into topics with separate sections
concentrating, for example, on 'The Road', 'You and
Your Car', 'Road Signs' and so on. In this way, you can
get a close insight into each major factor that makes up
the Highway Code and also into 'reading the road'
while driving. Additionally, each aspect can become
clear in your mind before you go on to the next.

Naturally, there are cross-over points between
sections. You will, for instance, find questions on 'The
Road' repeated, in different form, in questions on 'Road
Signs'. Such repetition can itself be an aid to learning
and afterwards you can select questions at random, and
so rehearse the Highway Code section of your driving
test. There is also an index to help you locate questions
on particular aspects which you may wish to revise.

All this aims, firstly, to acquaint you with matters of
law relating to the use of the road, such as where you
may or may not park. Secondly, it aims to concentrate
your attention on the business of driving while using
your own common sense and awareness of safety and
consideration for others. Finally, it aims to teach you
the language of the road, that is, the meaning of its
signs, signals and various markings. As well as being
the aims of this book, these are, of course, the basic
purposes of the Highway Code as well.

# Metrication Chart

In the Highway Code published by Her Majesty's Stationery Office, in the current, revised 1985 version, some weights, measures and distances can be found both in metric form and in non-metric form. For your guidance, therefore, here is a conversion table of basic measures.

| Non-metric | Metric |
|---|---|
| 1 foot | 0.3048 metres |
| 1 yard = 3 feet | 0.9144 metres |
| 1 mile | 1.6093 kilometres |
| 1 pound [lb.] | 0.4536 kilogrammes |
| 1 ton | 1.016 tonnes |

| Metric | Non-metric |
|---|---|
| 1 Metre | 1.094 yards [ = 3.282 feet] |
| 1 Kilometre | 0.62137 mile |
| 1 Kilogramme | 2.2046 pounds [lb.] |
| 1 Tonne | 0.9842 ton |

# Section One
# The Road

**1.** How close to the car in front of you may you drive, as a general rule of safety on the road?

**2.** You are driving along the road at a safe cruising speed when a vehicle overtakes you and moves into the gap between your car and the car in front. What should you do?

**3.** When driving along a fogbound road, what is your stopping distance?

**4.** On a dry road, in good driving conditions, what is the minimum stopping distance for a car going at the following speeds?

a] 60 mph.

b] 40 mph.

c] 30 mph.

**5.** In the Highway Code, shortest or minimum stopping distances comprise THINKING and BRAKING distances added together. What is the THINKING DISTANCE for a motorist who has to stop when driving at the following speeds?

a] 70 mph.

b] 50 mph.

c] 30 mph.

**6.** What is the BRAKING DISTANCE for a car going at 40 mph?

**7.** When driving at 20 mph, the shortest stopping distance is 40 feet. How is this divided between THINKING and BRAKING distances?

**8.** When a bus in front of you indicates that it is about to move out from a bus stop, what should you do (allowing that it is safe to do so)?

**9.** What is the first and most important requirement a motorist must observe when driving in fog?

**10.** Can you name two particular disadvantages from which cyclists suffer when on the road?

**11.** What can you do to prevent yourself from becoming sleepy when driving on a long journey or when driving on the motorway?

**12.** At what speed in mph is the BRAKING DISTANCE twice the THINKING DISTANCE before your car comes to a halt?

**13.** In fog, what should you do if a vehicle comes up close behind you, close enough, let us say, to 'fill' your rear-view mirror? Should you speed up, for instance?

**14.** In wet and slippery road conditions, how can you quickly and easily reckon the appropriate gap between your car and the car in front of you?

**15.** In Britain and some other countries, drivers normally drive on the left of the road. However, you are sometimes permitted to drive on the right. Can you name at least three situations in which you can do this?

**16.** There are stationary vehicles and some pedestrians at the side of a road along which you are driving. What should you do when you drive past them?

**17.** Name three people who are authorised to direct or signal instructions to cars on the road.

**18.** When carrying loads on your car or vehicle or towing loads, what is the most important aspect to remember and check?

**19.** A lane control signal over a road has four small box panels, two of which show white downward pointing arrows. Three of the box panels show red 'X's. How many lanes are open on this road?

**20.** A green direction sign indicates a roundabout from which roads are shown leading to four destinations. How many exits/entrances are there on this roundabout?

**21.** What does 'R' printed on a white, black-edged road sign mean?

**22.** On the road surface, how are traffic lanes indicated by markings?

**23.** You see a long, horizontal, black sign with white chevrons pointing to the right. What does this tell you about the road ahead?

**24.** You are approaching a set of traffic lights. What is indicated if they show the following?

a] An amber light on its own.

b] Red and amber lights together.

c] A red light with a green filter arrow pointing left.

**25.** You are not allowed to stop on a motorway except when your car breaks down and you can't help it, or in an emergency such as stopping in order to prevent an accident. Name three other circumstances in which you can stop on a motorway.

**26.** What is the deceleration lane on a motorway?

**27.** You are driving along a motorway when you see that the overhead panel above your lane is showing a lighted arrow. This indicates a turn to the left. What does this mean?

**28.** Special signs on motorways advise you of road conditions ahead. How do these signs tell you that normal conditions prevail?

**29.** There is a flashing amber signal on the motorway. What is it telling you?

**30.** You are driving along a motorway, heading for your holiday destination. Your family's luggage is stowed on the roof of your car when suddenly a suitcase falls off and lands on the road. You should stop immediately and go back to retrieve it. *TRUE* or *FALSE*?

**31.** When you are driving along a road, in what circumstances are you permitted to switch on your hazard warning lights?

**32.** Your car has broken down on the road. To warn other drivers, at what distance should you place your reflecting red triangle warning sign...

a] On an ordinary road (for instance, an A or B road)?

b] On a motorway?

# Section Two
# Other Road Users

**1.** According to the Highway Code, what is the definition of a Heavy Goods Vehicle?

**2.** Describe the markings carried at the back of Heavy Goods Vehicles to warn other road users of their presence.

**3.** How many signal lights do you use to indicate to other drivers and road users that you are moving or turning to the left or right?

**4.** What hand signals do you use when you wish to inform drivers behind you that you are about to turn left or move left?

**5.** At Zebra crossings, how do you let pedestrians know you are about to stop for them?

**6.** Broken, thick white lines are painted across carriageways to indicate those places where you must give way to other traffic. Which of the following white lines appear at *ROUNDABOUTS*?

a] Small, box-like, white rectangles painted close together.

b] Two parallel lines of longer white rectangles painted fairly close together.

c] A single line of longer white rectangles spaced their own width apart on the road.

**7.** Which white, black-edged, rectangular sign indicates a bus lane on the road at the junction ahead?

**8.** A sign indicating a parking place for caravans shows a caravan in silhouette and one other feature. What is it?

**9.** Which road sign indicates a route that is recommended for pedal cyclists?.

**10.** State, in general terms, when you should look into your rear-view mirror while driving.

**11.** You are riding a motorcycle and want to overtake. Before doing so, what *TWO* actions must you take?

**12.** You are driving a car and want to overtake the vehicle in front. What action must you take before doing so – and for what purpose?

**13.** The road conditions are good. The road is dry and the sun is shining, but fortunately not into your eyes. How should you make a quick reckoning of the proper gap between your car and the car in front of you?

**14.** Name three types of emergency vehicle for which you should always make way on the road.

**15.** Which of the followed is permitted to drive in the *RIGHT HAND LANE* of a carriageway with three or more lanes?

a] A bus 9 metres long.

b] A bus 12 metres long or more.

c] A vehicle towing a trailer.

d] A goods vehicle with operating weight of 5 tonnes.

e] A vehicle with operating weight of more than $7\frac{1}{2}$ tonnes.

**16.** You have overtaken a car on the motorway. What should your next move be?

**17.** What does it mean if you see a vehicle flashing blue lights or hear one sounding two-tone horns or sirens, or bells?

**18.** You are driving along a road in fairly heavy traffic. Some distance in front, on the left-hand side of your lane, you see two people riding horses. Each rider has only one hand on the bridle of their own horse. With the other, they are holding the bridles of horses which they are leading. As you drive past the two riders, which horses – those being ridden or those being led – should be nearer to you?

**19.** Why should motorists be particularly watchful when herds of animals are being moved along roads with bends or which follow contours of hills?

**20.** Which of the following are not permitted to use motorways?

a] Combine harvesters.   d] Motorcyclists.
b] Learner drivers.      e] Pedestrians.
c] Pedal cyclists.

**21.** You notice a hitchhiker on the slip road at the approach to a motorway and want to give him a lift. Can you?

**22.** You are driving along a road with a gentle bend to the left ahead. It is after sunset and you can't see the other road users who are just rounding the bend very clearly. However, you *can* see a white light being carried in front and a red light also being carried a little way behind. These lights tell you who or what is using the road at that point. So who or what are they?

**23.** You see a car a little way ahead, pulled in at the side of the road with its hazard warning lights flashing. The car has not broken down, so what else could the driver be doing?

**24.** You have reached your destination and have parked by the side of the road in the correct position. You move to open your car door to get out, but what must you do first?

**25.** Particularly when driving at night, you should always take care that your headlights do not dazzle other drivers. It is not, however, just a matter of dipping your headlights when other drivers are around. In which of the following situations should you dip your headlamps?

a] When driving on a lighted motorway or other high speed road.

b] When driving through a lighted road in a built-up area.

c] When the light from your headlamps can reach the driver of the vehicle in front of you.

d] When another vehicle approaches from the opposite direction.

**26.** In what circumstances are you permitted to flash your headlamps?

**27.** In what circumstances can you sound the horn on your car?

**28.** A vehicle is approaching from the right and is signalling with its left-hand indicator. Should you drive on past it?

**29.** As a general rule, on which side of the vehicle in front should you overtake?

**30.** What two elements must you watch out for when entering or driving out of a property which borders on a road?

**31.** What is the purpose of a Zebra crossing?

**32.** Pedestrians are standing by the side of the road, waiting to cross. You intend to slow down and let them traverse the road but should not signal to them to do so. Why?

**33.** You come upon zig zag lines on either side of the driving lane, marked in the road. What lies ahead?

**34.** Name three ways in which pedestrian crossings may be controlled.

**35.** When a Pelican pedestrian crossing has a central refuge, does this count as two separate crossings?

**36.** What is written on the sign used by School Crossing Patrols?

**37.** You are first on the scene of an accident. What information should you particularly note in order to give the details to the police and ambulance authorities?

**38.** When approaching a level crossing, do you stop *ONLY* when the red STOP signs light up on the barrier or gate between the road and the railway?

**39.** You see the letters HR on a local direction sign (a rectangular panel with yellow background and black lettering). Who would you expect to find using the road with this sign?

**40.** Diamond-shaped information panels are carried by vehicles containing dangerous goods or substances.

The panels include wording and a picture symbol in each case, *viz.*, TOXIC, with a skull and crossbones depicted above it, on a plain white diamond. What picture symbol is used to denote the following?

a] Spontaneously combustible (substance).
b] Oxidising agent.
c] Compressed gas.
d] Radioactive (substance).
e] Corrosive (substance).

**41.** The diamond-shaped panels indicating dangerous substances have their own colour or colour combinations. Match the colouring to the wording and symbol.

| | |
|---|---|
| a] Toxic. | i] White above, black below. |
| b] Spontaneously combustible. | ii] White above, red below. |
| c] Compressed gas. | iii] Plain white. |
| d] Radioactive. | iv] Green. |
| e] Corrosive substance. | v] Yellow. |
| f] Oxidising substance. | |

**42.** When the load on a vehicle overhangs the front or the rear of the vehicle by more than 1.83 metres, an additional projection marker must be carried. Describe this projection marker.

**43.** Yellow, red-edged, rectangular plates are fitted to Long Vehicles and the plates says exactly that. What does this sign also tell you, by inference?

# Section Three
# Driving Conditions and
# Night Driving

**1.** A red-edged, white, triangular sign warns of a ford in the road ahead. What does the sign show?

**2.** Are you allowed to let your vehicle wait in the following places?

a] In the area of zig zag lines on either side of a Zebra crossing.

b] On the right-hand side of a one-way street at night.

c] In the zone indicated by rows of studs on the approach to a Pelican crossing, when a pedestrian is crossing the road.

d] On the left-hand side of the road at night.

e] In a bus lane.

f] Where the verges of a section of road are not marked by white lines.

g] At bus stops marked by wide yellow lines at 6 a.m..

**3.** In a built-up area, can you sound your car horn at these times?

a] Between 9.30 p.m. and midnight?

b] Between 6 a.m. and 6 p.m.?

c] Between 7 a.m. and 11.30 p.m.?

d] At no time.

**4.** On a dry road, in good conditions, you are going at a good pace in a de-restricted area. Suddenly you have to stop and you do so in the minimum stopping distance of 240 feet. What was your speed?

**5.** Where road conditions are wet or slippery, what should the minimum stopping distance for your car relative to its speed be?

a] At least trebled.

b] At least doubled.

c] At least quadrupled.

**6.** When may vehicles other than buses use a specially designated bus lane?

**7.** When overtaking, what special difficulties must you bear in mind when conditions are foggy or misty, or when it is dusk or night-time?

**8.** You find yourself in a traffic queue and want to move into another lane on the road in order to avoid the traffic jam. Is it permitted to do this?

**9.** You are about to turn into a road at a junction. What should you particularly look out for on the road into which you are turning?

**10.** On a motorway, the special signs which give information about road conditions are blank. What does this signify?

**11.** On some motorways, amber signals may be used to denote slippery roads ahead or foggy conditions. Describe how the signals operate.

**12.** You see a long, horizontal, black sign ahead with white chevrons pointing to the left. What does this tell you about the road ahead?

**13.** You see a sign (a white, red-edged triangle) showing an exclamation mark in black. What does it mean?

**14.** Describe the overhead motorway sign which means

*DO NOT MOVE FURTHER ALONG THIS LANE.*

**15.** You are on a level crossing when, suddenly you realise that the amber warning lights on the automatic half-barrier are showing and you can hear the alarm. From these signals, you know a train is approaching. What should you do?

**16.** You wish to turn right from a side road into a dual carriageway, but the central reservation is too narrow for your vehicle to pause there safely. What should you do?

**17.** You come upon a herd of animals being led along the road. What should you particularly avoid doing in these circumstances?

**18.** What is the significance of a single broken line, with long markings and short gaps in the middle of the road?

**19.** If you are driving a large or slow-moving vehicle and wish to pass over a level crossing, how do you ensure it is safe to do so?

**20.** At an 'open' level crossing, how can you make sure that there are no trains approaching?

**21.** In an area where you are permitted to park your vehicle at night without lights, what is the minimum distance you should park it from a road junction?

**22.** If your car breaks down at night, why is it inadvisable to stand at the rear of the vehicle?

**23.** Automatic 'open' level crossings have amber lights followed by flashing red STOP lights. If a train passes over the crossing but the lights continue to flash, what does this mean?

**24.** Where a vehicle is permitted to park at night without lights, should you place it facing or opposing the direction of the traffic on the road?

**25.** Suppose you come upon an accident involving a vehicle carrying dangerous goods – what additional information (apart from the fact of the accident) should you report to the emergency services?

**26.** What is the significance of a pedestrian carrying a white stick with two red, reflectorised bands?

**27.** Young people under 15 and older people over 60 may share a potentially dangerous characteristic. What is it?

**28.** What is the first and most important requirement when driving in fog?

**29.** In what conditions should you calculate the proper gap between your car and the car in front at two yards for every mile per hour of your speed?

**30.** You are following a car at a safe distance when a vehicle comes up behind you and moves in too close for comfort. Your natural urge is to increase your own speed in order to get away from the car behind. Should you follow your natural urge?

**31.** When an information sign shows a short, horizontal, *RED* bar across a line indicating a route, what does this mean?

**32.** Why are vehicles prohibited from waiting or parking near or at a bend in the road, on the brow of a hill or on a hump-backed bridge?

**33.** When should you use your headlamps, not your sidelights, while driving at night?

a] On roads with no street lighting.
b] Where the street lamps are not alight.
c] Where street lamps are more than 50 yards apart.
d] Where there are no street lamps.
e] Where visibility is reduced – perhaps by fog – to less than 300 metres.

**34.** Tinted spectacles worn while driving can help cut out sunshine glare, but are you allowed to wear them at night?

**35.** Two triangular, red-edged, white signs warn of the road narrowing ahead. Both comprise two parallel lines, but in one the right-hand line has an inward kink. In the other, both lines kink towards each other. What do each of these signs indicate?

**36.** What road sign indicates the presence of wild animals in the vicinity?

# Section Four
# Motorways, Primary
# Routes and Local Roads

## Motorways

**1.** What sign is used to indicate the start of a motorway?

**2.** What is the most noticeable difference between signs on motorways and those on other roads, such as primary or local roads?

**3.** A motorway sign shows 'M10 (M1)'. What does this signify?

**4.** On the motorway, you are allowed to overtake...

a] In a lane on the left.
b] On the hard shoulder.
*TRUE* or *FALSE*?

**5.** What is the purpose of the fast lane on the motorway?

**6.** Studs on the motorway have various colours depending on their purpose. Match up the location of the studs to their colours in the following lists:

**Locations**

a] The left-hand side of the motorway.
b] The right-hand side of the motorway.
c] The line separating the acceleration and deceleration lanes from the through carriageway.

**Stud colours**

i]  Amber.
ii]  Red.
iii] Green.

**7.** Can you reverse your car on the motorway?

**8.** Except when overtaking, you must drive in the left-hand lane on motorways with...

a] Three lanes.
b] Two lanes.
*TRUE* or *FALSE*?

**9.** Where are you allowed to let your vehicle stand on the motorway in an emergency?

**10.** On which side of the motorway will you find the exit slip road that takes you back to the 'ordinary' road system?

**11.** What lighted signal would you expect to find on an overhead panel on the motorway telling you to leave the motorway at the next exit?

**12.** It is important that you regularly look at your speedometer when driving on the motorway. Why?

**13.** You have broken down on the motorway and have managed to get your car onto the hard shoulder. How do you find the nearest telephone in order to inform the authorities?

**14.** The distance to exits from the motorway are indicated by panels showing three, then two, then one white bar in a rectangular light blue panel. How many yards to the exit does each white bar represent?

**15.** On a motorway, an overhead signal in your lane shows a lighted arrow pointing diagonally downwards to the left. What does this mean?

# Primary Routes and Local Roads

**1.** Describe the road markings which indicate the edges of lanes on the road.

**2.** How do you move your arm when signalling that you want to move or turn to the right?

**3.** What are you indicating when you extend your arm and move it rapidly up and down?

**4.** A police officer is directing the traffic. You signal to the officer by showing him the palm of your upraised left hand. What are you saying about your driving intentions?

**5.** What does it signify if a police officer directing traffic faces the traffic with his arm straight up?

**6.** *Local* direction signs, which are white panels, have borders that are which colour?

a] Red.

b] Green.

c] Light blue.

d] Yellow.

e] They have no borders.

**7.** At a road junction, the traffic lights have turned green. Does this *invariably* mean that you can drive on?

**8.** You reach a road junction on a three-lane section of a primary road. The traffic lights at the junction are showing green and so is a filter arrow indicating a left turn. In which lane should you be if you want to drive straight on?

**9.** You want to make a right turn from a main road. However, another vehicle coming from the opposite direction, also wishes to do so. This means you will have to pass the other vehicle as you prepare to make your own right turn. When passing the other vehicle, should you keep it to your left or to your right?

**10.** Where should you wait when turning right from a dual carriageway?

**11.** In which of the following circumstances, if any, are you allowed to overtake on the *LEFT-HAND SIDE*?

a] On dual carriageways.

b] In one-way streets.

c] When a queue of traffic in a lane to your right is moving more slowly than you are.

d] If you want to turn left.

20

**12.** You see a white, black-edged sign with the letter 'R' in it. What does the sign denote?

**13.** What can you deduce from the fact that red and amber traffic lights are showing together?

**14.** An eight-sided, red sign says STOP in white letters. A white, red-edged, inverted triangle says GIVE WAY in black letters. What do these two road signs have in common?

**15.** A roundabout has four exits. You wish to take the third. At what point should you indicate your intention?

**16.** Can you reverse from a side road into a main road?

**17.** What is the purpose of giving signals while driving?

**18.** You are driving slowly and carefully along a narrow, winding road. There is a great deal of oncoming traffic. A faster vehicle than yours comes up behind you and wants to overtake. What should you do?

**19.** When should you use your rear fog lamps?

a] At night.
b] When it is misty.
c] When it is raining.
d] When it is foggy.

**20.** When reversing, should you undo your seat belt or keep it fastened?

**21.** At an automatic, 'open', level crossing, what signal do the lights give that it is safe to cross?

**22.** What is an automatic, half-barrier level crossing? And how would you describe the half-barrier?

**23.** Out in the countryside, you are driving along a narrow single-track road when a vehicle comes towards you. There is a passing place at this point, but it is not on your side of the road. What should you do?

**24.** At a junction leading into a main road where there are broken white lines in front of your car, in which road do vehicles have the right of way?

**25.** On a three-lane dual carriageway, what is the purpose of the right-hand lane?

**26.** In what circumstances are you allowed to drive in the centre lane on a three-lane dual carriageway, and for how long?

**27.** You are driving along a one-way street and wish to turn off it at the next exit on the right. How do you prepare to make this manoeuvre?

**28.** If you have to move from one lane to another on the road, what must you normally do before starting this manoeuvre?

a] Accelerate.
b] Glance in your mirror.
c] Sound your horn.
d] Use your signal indicators.

**29.** On a single carriageway or undivided road, where there are three lanes, which lane is used...

a] For overtaking?
b] For right turns?

# Section Five
# You and Your Car

**1.** According to the Highway Code, by how much can the wearing of a seat belt reduce the risk of death or injury in an accident?

**2.** At what age can a young person legally wear an adult seat belt?

**3.** What type of clothing should motor cyclists and other cyclists wear when on the road?

**4.** You have a well-behaved and obedient dog in the car with you. Can you let it out on a road without a lead?

**5.** What is the safest place for a young child when travelling in a car?

**6.** If your car is fitted with L-plates, perhaps while a friend or relative is occasionally using it to learn how to drive, what should you do when your car is *NOT* being used for learning or practising? Can you leave the L-plates as fitted or should you remove them?

**7.** Who is required *by law* to wear a seat belt when travelling by car?

**8.** You are required, as a driver, to wear your seat belt when reversing your car. *TRUE* or *FALSE*?

**9.** What are the most important requirements in choosing an approved 'child-restraint' or seat belt?

**10.** A child-restraint or seat belt is one protection you can give a youngster travelling by car. Can you think of another?

**11.** You wish to warn other road users of your presence. Which two methods are open to you for this purpose?

**12.** You should not drive a car while under the influence of alcohol or drugs. Name two other conditions of health or lack of well-being which make it inadvisable to drive.

**13.** The headlamps on your car should always be properly adjusted. Name the principal *SAFETY* reason for this.

**14.** You are going on holiday and travelling by car. What road sign should you watch out for when you wish to find a nearby Holiday Route?

**15.** A police officer is directing traffic. You are waiting for instructions at the side of the road. The police officer stands sideways on to the traffic and beckons to you with upraised arm. What is he telling you to do?

**16.** You wind down the driver's window, extend your arm and make a circular movement with it. What are you saying to other drivers?

**17.** If you extend your arm from the driver's window and hold it there, without moving it, what are you telling other drivers?

**18.** A police officer is controlling the traffic and you wish to tell him that you want to drive straight on. How do you do this?

**19.** What should you do if you become tired on a long journey and your concentration begins to falter?

**20.** You are driving along the road and want to turn right. You glance into your rear-view mirror and see that it is safe to turn right, then, just as you are preparing to make the manoeuvre, you realise you have forgotten to do something. What is it?

**21.** You have parked by the side of the road, in the correct position. You have made sure the handbrake is on firmly and that the engine and headlamps are switched off. What else should you do to ensure the safety of your car?

**22.** There are eight items in your car to which you should give particular attention. According to the Highway Code, they must be in first-class condition at all times. Six of these items are lights, brakes, steering, seat belts, de-misters and washers. What are the other two?

**23.** Why is it particularly important to ensure that any loads you carry or tow are securely tied on?

**24.** You wish to draw to the side of the road in order to make a delivery. What signals in your car should you switch on for this purpose?

**25.** You have parked your car, but just as you are about to open the door to get out, you see a pedal cyclist approaching behind you. What should you do?

**26.** What happens when you switch on the hazard warning device in your car?

**27.** Your car has broken down, at night, on the motorway. You manage to get your car to the hard shoulder, then get out your reflecting red triangle warning sign and place it 50 yards away from your car. You telephone the police, but when they arrive, they look at the warning sign and frown. What have you done wrong?

**28.** Which of your car's facilities should you especially use when driving in fog?

**29.** You are driving at 45 mph. The conditions are good but there is a car in front of you. Being a good driver, with a thorough knowledge of the Highway Code, you have placed your car at the proper distance between your car and the one in front. How far away from the car in front are you driving?

**30.** You should always drive round bends in the road with care, but why should you be especially alert when the bend goes to the left?

# Section Six
# Markings on the Road

**1.** What road marking indicates a bus stop?

**2.** How are traffic lanes indicated by road markings?

**3.** You see KEEP CLEAR painted on the road in tall white letters. What is it that you must keep clear?

**4.** A road marking consists of zig zag yellow lines. Written between the lines are three words.

.... Keep Clear

What is the first word and what does the road marking indicate?

**5.** What type of roundabout has (at places where you must give way to traffic already on it) a line of small, box-shaped rectangles painted on the road?

**6.** There are two kinds of STOP lines painted across the carriageway. One is for stopping at a STOP sign. The other is for stopping at traffic signals or a police control. How do these two stop lines differ?

**7.** Yellow lines painted over the kerb are accompanied by an explanatory plate nearby. How many lines would you expect to see on the kerb if the plate forbad the following.

a] Loading at any time.
b] Loading outside normal working hours (i.e. 9.30 a.m. – 4.30 p.m.).
c] Loading after 8.30 a.m. or before 6.30 p.m. on working days, including Saturdays.

**8.** Describe the road markings which indicate the edges of driving lanes.

**9.** You are in a side road, waiting to enter the main road and, of course, you are giving way to the traffic on the main road. There is a line of markings on the road to tell you where to wait. Describe this line.

**10.** Yellow lines indicate certain restrictions. What type of restrictions are indicated by yellow lines painted on the road and what type by yellow lines painted on the kerb?

**11.** Two types of yellow line marking, with short crossbars at each end, are used to indicate No Waiting for at least eight hours between 7 a.m. and 7 p.m. on four or more weekdays. One comprises a single yellow line, the other a double yellow line. Which of these two *ALSO* prohibits waiting on additional periods before 7 a.m. and after 7 p.m.?

**12.** Describe the road markings which indicate the centre of the road.

**13.** You see a white triangle with a thick base and the triangle point facing towards you, painted on the road. What lies ahead?

**14.** Describe the marking on the road which tells you that there is a GIVE WAY place just ahead.

**15.** When white diagonal stripes or white chevrons are painted on the road, their purpose is . . .

a] To separate streams of traffic on the road.
b] To indicate overtaking areas.
c] To indicate where traffic may turn right.

**16.** Under what circumstances are you permitted to cross a double white line when the line nearer to you is a *solid* one?

a] When overtaking.
b] When moving out of premises or a side road.
c] To avoid a stationary obstruction in the road.
d] None.

**17.** Of the two lines in the centre of the road, the broken white line is nearer to you. Can you overtake here and so cross the white lines?

**18.** What road markings indicate the approach to a Zebra crossing?

**19.** Roads may have coloured reflective studs embedded in them. What is indicated by studs in the following colours?

a] Amber.
b] Red.
c] White.
d] Green.

**20.** You have seen the markings painted on the road which indicate a Zebra crossing ahead and you want to overtake. Should you?

**21.** You would obviously not drive across a Zebra crossing while pedestrians are actually on it, but can you drive over it when pedestrians are at the kerb by the crossing?

**22.** On the motorway, what is indicated by green studs embedded in the road surface?

**23.** On the motorway, what is indicated by red studs embedded in the road surface?

**24.** A chevron painted in the road has a solid white-edged line. Are you allowed to drive over it at any time?

**25.** Where in the road may you see white studs used in conjunction with the lines?

# Section Seven
# Signs on the Road

**1.** Describe the shape of the majority of warning signs you may see on the road.

**2.** A round, white, red-edged sign shows the figure of a man walking. What does this sign denote?

**3.** There are two arrows in a triangular sign which indicate that there is two-way traffic going across a one-way road. Describe the two arrows.

**4.** When a sign shows red, amber and green traffic lights in a vertical rectangle, with a red bar diagonally across them, what does this mean?

**5.** A white, red-edged sign shows two cars, a black one on the left, a red one on the right. What does this signify?

**6.** What sign, in the form of a diamond-shaped panel, must be carried by vehicles loaded with spontaneously combustible materials?

**7.** Vehicles with loads that overhang the front or rear by more than 1.83 metres must carry triangular projection markers with red- and white-slanted stripes. They come in two shapes...
a] A long, right-angled triangle.
b] An isosceles triangle (i.e. with sides of equal length) pointing downwards.
Which of them is carried on the *SIDE* of the vehicle and which at the *REAR*?

**8.** Where are you likely to see a panel showing alternating flashing red light signals, indicating that you must stop?

**9.** What is the nature of the majority of circular signs with red edges?

**10.** When a circular blue sign shows a bicycle on the left and an adult and child pedestrians on the right, what does this mean?

**11.** A stretch of road has, firstly, a blue sign showing '30' written in white. Further on, there is another sign – the same one, in fact, but with a red diagonal bar across the '30'. What do the two signs mean and on what kind of road are you most likely to find them?

**12.** A level crossing sign comprises a large blue panel above a smaller, white one. The blue panel says:
 'DRIVERS OF LARGE OR SLOW VEHICLES MUST . . .'
Complete the instruction.

**13.** On the blue level crossing panel mentioned in Question 12 above, what speed is mentioned as being 'slow' for vehicles?

**14.** How many panels make up the sign at a level crossing with low ground clearance, and what is shown on the top sign?

**15.** Which circular blue road sign contains the following?

a] Two arrows.
b] Three arrows.

**16.** Two triangular, red-edged signs indicate a level crossing ahead. One of them contains the silhouette of a gate. The other contains the silhouette of a steam engine. What is the chief difference between level crossings displaying one or other of these signs?

**17.** What does the silhouette of an aircraft mean on a road sign, and what *shape* is the sign?

**18.** Describe the colours in which you may expect to find direction signs on non-primary routes, such as B roads?

**19.** How does a road sign tell you that it indicates a 'Ring Road'?

**20.** What is the significance of a yellow panel printed with a black motif – an arrowhead pointing left or right?

**21.** What is indicated by white arrows on a blue background when they are displayed on a long black panel over a motorway?

**22.** A white, red-edged, round sign shows the outline of a car front. Does this mean that no vehicles are allowed on the road?

**23.** How does a road sign indicate an unspecified danger lying ahead?

**24.** What can you infer from a triangular, red-edged road sign showing a deer in silhouette?

**25.** What colour is the border around the white panels which are used for local direction signs?

**26.** A local road direction sign indicates, at the junction just ahead one destination marked by an arrow pointing upwards and another with an arrow pointing left. Describe the junction and the roads leading into and out of it.

**27.** Information signs on the road are all rectangular. *TRUE* or *FALSE*?

**28.** Describe the information sign indicating a parking meter zone.

**29.** What is the import of a flashing amber signal, placed below the sign which indicates, in advance, that there is a school crossing patrol in operation ahead?

**30.** A road has four lanes. There are four, small, box panels placed over the road which indicate that two of the lanes are open and the other two closed. What would you expect to find displayed in the box panels?

**31.** Describe the sign which indicates a parking place for caravans.

**32.** What does a large white 'H' on a light blue background denote when displayed on a road sign?

**33.** A sign on a motorway shows two white bars in a rectangular light blue panel. How far is the sign from the next motorway exit?

**34.** A rectangular road sign with a pale blue background shows a 'T' shape motif. The vertical shaft of the 'T' is painted in white, the cross-bar of the 'T' in red. What does this mean?

**35.** Describe the roadside sign on a three-lane motorway which means RIGHT-HAND LANE CLOSED.

**36.** Describe the overhead motorway sign which means END OF RESTRICTION.

**37.** The overhead signal above your lane on the motorway is flashing a set of red lights. What should you do?

**38.** What is signified by a red light showing on a level crossing?

**39.** What is signified by two pairs of alternating flashing red lights on an overhead motorway sign?

**40.** A large, white, square road sign has a white 'P' on the left-hand side, enclosed in a light blue square. What does the rest of the sign say? (Three words.)

**41.** What can you expect to see in a long, horizontal, black road sign which indicates a sharp bend in the road to the left?

**42.** On a level crossing with automatic barriers a plain, white, square sign says ...

'AUTOMATIC BARRIERS. STOP WHEN ...'
Complete the sentence. (Two words.)

**43.** A triangular, red-edged sign shows the road ahead as a straight line with another line indicating a line of traffic merging with it from the left. Which line of traffic has priority?

**44.** A level crossing that does not have a barrier shows its usual white, diagonal cross with red edges. However, the lower half of the cross is reproduced *BELOW* the full cross. What does this mean?

**45.** What sign indicates a roundabout ahead?

**46.** Name two triangular, red-edged signs which show silhouettes of people.

**47.** A triangular, red-edged sign on a road shows two parallel lines which kink inwards, towards each other. What does this mean?

**48.** Two blue signs on the road feature arrows pointing straight up. One blue sign is round, the other is rectangular. What does each signify?

# Section Eight
# Roundabouts and Level Crossings

**1.** What is the purpose of a roundabout?

**2.** Describe a 'mini' roundabout.

**3.** Some very large roundabouts have a series of 'mini' roundabouts surrounding them. What is the purpose of such a system and how does traffic move on it?

**4.** Who has the right of way on a roundabout?

**5.** What is the first thing you must do when you reach a roundabout?

**6.** Are the rules for driving on roundabouts on ordinary roads different from those on motorways and on dual carriageways?

**7.** When you are waiting to enter a roundabout, traffic already on the roundabout will be moving from which direction?

a] Left to right in front of you.

b] Right to left in front of you.

**8.** A roundabout has four exits and you wish to take the third one. As you drive past the second exit, you signal that you are about to turn left into this third exit. Have you done the right thing?

**9.** If there are two lanes at the entrance to a roundabout, for *what purpose* do you approach in . . .

a] The left-hand lane?

b] The right-hand lane?

**10.** What is an 'open' level crossing?

**11.** At an automatic level crossing, you find amber lights followed by flashing red STOP lights. You of course halt and let the train that is on the line pass over the crossing. Once it has gone, however, the lights continue to flash. Should you drive over the crossing at this juncture?

**12.** If the lights go out on an automatic level crossing, what does this signify?

**13.** A level crossing has an automatic barrier across the left-hand side of the road only. What kind of a crossing is this?

**14.** Certain level crossings have no gates or barriers, no attendants or red lights, but they *do* have a sign. What does the sign say?

**15.** Automatic half-barrier level crossings have three signals indicating, between them, that vehicles must stop at the crossing. Amber lights and flashing red STOP lights are two of these signals. What is the third and when does it occur?

**16.** What should you do if you approach a level crossing and see the barrier is descending or the gates are just beginning to close?

**17.** On which type of level crossing would you expect to find a barrier with red and white horizontal stripes?

**18.** You see, from a sign on the road, that there is a level crossing ahead. The sign shows a steam engine in silhouette. What type of level crossing is ahead?

**19.** Level crossings without barriers show a white diagonal cross with red edges. How do you know, by looking at this cross, whether the crossing is used by ...

a] One railway line?
b] Two or more railway lines?

**20.** At level crossings which have automatic barriers there is a plain, white, square sign. On it is written an instruction ...
'..... Stop when lights show'.
How does the instruction begin? (Two words.)

**21.** What sign on the road indicates that there is a roundabout ahead?

**22.** A triangular, red-edged sign at a level crossing shows the silhouette of a gate. What type of crossing is this?

**23.** What picture could you expect to see indicating a level crossing with a barrier?

**24.** An open level crossing has a set of four signs, one below the other. At the top, there is a white, red-edged, diagonal cross. At the bottom, there is a small, red and white, diagonal-striped panel. Describe the two signs in between.

**25.** At a level crossing, you see a panel showing alternating, flashing, red light signals, indicating that you must stop. This is not the only place you may see such a sign. Can you name two others?

**26.** You are in the course of going over a level crossing when the amber warning lights on the crossing start to show and you hear the accompanying alarm. What should you do?

a] Reverse your car off the crossing.
b] Stay where you are.
c] Drive forwards off the crossing.

**27.** When there are several lanes at the entrance to a roundabout, can you use any of them as you approach?

**28.** Once on the roundabout, which lane should you use to drive on and round it?

**29.** Traffic on roundabouts moves in an anti-clockwise direction. *TRUE* or *FALSE*?

**30.** You enter a roundabout and want to take the first exit from it. What signal do you give and when do you give it?

**31.** Assuming that it is clear for you to do so, in what lane on the road should you approach a roundabout?

**32.** In what circumstances will you signal, firstly, *RIGHT* and then, *LEFT* on a roundabout?

**33.** What warning signal at a level crossing tells you that a train is approaching?

**34.** At an 'open' level crossing, that is, one without gates or barriers, you should make sure that no trains are approaching by listening for the sound of a train and *two* other actions. What are these?

**35.** You approach a level crossing with a barrier across the left-hand side of the road only. What type of level crossing is this?

**36.** If you are driving a large and/or slow-moving vehicle and wish to traverse a level crossing, how do you ensure that it is safe to do so?

**37.** A slow-moving vehicle, as defined by signs at level crossings, drives at a maximum speed. What speed?

a] 20 mph.
b] 12 mph.
c] 5 mph.

**38.** At a level crossing, when the top sign of a three-part warning sign shows two humps in a white, red-edged triangle, what does this mean?

**39.** At a level crossing, where are the familiar 'Red–Amber–Green' traffic lights placed?

**40.** When on a roundabout, other vehicles will cross in front of you when taking exits before your own. What should you do when this occurs?

# Section Nine
# Parking and Waiting

**1.** There is a parked vehicle in your lane a short way ahead of you. Another vehicle is coming towards you from the opposite direction. Should you move out and drive past the parked vehicle or not?

**2.** Disabled persons are entitled to certain parking concessions such as specially designated bays in multi-storey car parks which serve a supermarket. Disabled drivers must display a badge in their car so that other drivers will recognise them. What colour is the badge and where is it displayed?

**3.** A mobile shop or library is parked at the roadside and is serving customers. What or who must you watch out for in these circumstances when driving along this road?

**4.** Where can you park your car on a motorway?

**5.** Where are you allowed to wait with your car on the motorway?

**6.** There are several stationary vehicles by the left-hand side of the road. Before you drive past them, what action should you take in preparation?

**7.** Are you permitted to park near a school entrance or a level crossing?

**8.** What is a fire hydrant and what does it look like?

**9.** Vehicles are prohibited from waiting or parking near a bend in the road, or near a hump-back bridge, because this would make it difficult for other road users to see the road clearly. There is another feature on roads where parking or waiting is banned for the same reason. What is it?

**10.** Vehicles are also prohibited from parking at the entrance to a hospital, a police, fire or coastguard station. These entrances have a feature in common. What is it?

**11.** It is not permitted to park opposite a traffic island in the middle of a road. Why?

**12.** When a vehicle is temporarily parked because the driver is loading or unloading, how does the driver indicate this circumstance?

**13.** You have parked your car by the side of the road. Before you open the door to get out, what must you check on the road itself?

**14.** You are permitted to park your vehicle opposite or nearly opposite a stationary vehicle on the other side of the road, even though this may narrow the road. However, the narrowing of the road has strict limits and you must not park if, by doing so, you would narrow the road by more than the width of how many vehicles?

a] Four vehicles.    c] Three vehicles.
b] Two vehicles.

**15.** Before leaving your vehicle parked by the road, you should switch off the engine and headlamps and, finally, lock the car. What else needs to be done before you may leave your vehicle?

**16.** Under certain conditions when motorcycles, cars, goods vehicles of up to 30 cwt unladen and invalid carriages can be parked at night without lights on roads, what must be the speed limit?

a] 50 mph or less.    c] 30 mph or less.
b] 20 mph or less.

**17.** When parking near a road junction, at what minimum distance should you do so?

a] 20 yards.    c] 15 yards.
b] 20 feet.

**18.** You see a bus waiting at a bus stop, taking on passengers. It is some way ahead of you on your side of the road, but just as you approach the bus signals that it is about to start moving again. What should you do?

**19.** Here are some of the places where you may, or may not, be allowed to let your vehicle wait. In which of these places can you let it wait.

a] In the area of zig zag lines on either side of a Zebra crossing.
b] On the right-hand side of a one-way street at night.
c] In a bus lane.
d] At 6 a.m. at bus stops marked by a wide yellow line.

**20.** *TRUE* or *FALSE*? You may let your vehicle wait...

a] In the zone indicated by rows of studs on the approach to a Pelican crossing when a pedestrian is crossing the road.
b] On the left-hand side of the road at night.
c] Where the verges of a section of road are *NOT* marked by white lines.

**21.** You have parked your car and your dog is anxious to get out. So you open the door and let him leap onto the pavement. What have you done wrong?

**22.** The plate which indicates that one may *NEVER* wait at a certain spot consists of a light blue, red-edged circle with a red, diagonal bar on a yellow background. Below the circle is some lettering. What does it say?

**23.** Where there are waiting restrictions, the plates displayed to indicate this state of affairs may have yellow or light blue backgrounds. Which one of these backgrounds tells you that a *LIMITED* amount of waiting is permitted?

**24.** In certain places you will see yellow lines painted over the edge of the kerb. What type of restriction does this indicate?

**25.** Where are yellow lines painted in order to denote that there are waiting restrictions?

**26.** If you see three yellow lines painted over a kerb, what *specific* restriction does this indicate?

**27.** One yellow line painted over the kerb indicates no loading outside normal working hours. What are normal working hours in this context?

**28.** There is a yellow line marking in the road with short crossbars at each end. This indicates no waiting for ... hours between 7 a.m. and ... on ... days of the week. (Fill in the three gaps.)

**29.** You may park on the slip road leading to a motorway. *TRUE* or *FALSE*?

**30.** You may park on the central reservation of a motorway. *TRUE* or *FALSE*?

**31.** What is the purpose of a motorway services area and where, in relation to the motorway, can it be found?

**32.** Parking places are sometimes reserved for specific users, such as disabled drivers. Who else may be given the benefit of special parking places?

**33.** What is a Disc Zone?

**34.** At what distance from a level crossing are you allowed to let your vehicle stand?

**35.** If the pavement alongside a road is very wide – say four or five times wider than the normal pavement – are you allowed to park on it or let your vehicle wait there?

**36.** On a fast main road, specific places are set aside for motorists to park their cars or wait. What are they called?

**37.** Can you park or wait on a flyover?

**38.** You are permitted to park or wait in an underpass. *TRUE* or *FALSE*?

**39.** When parking by the roadside, where should you position your car?

**40.** You are not allowed to park or wait in places where your car would hold up traffic or block areas which may be used by emergency vehicles. These are among several similar prohibitions, but which of the two mentioned above would you contravene if you parked your car or waited in the following places?

a] Next to a fire hydrant.
b] In a tunnel.
c] By a doctor's premises.
d] In a passing place on a single-track road.

# Section Ten
# Breakdowns, Accidents and Mishaps

**1.** If your vehicle breaks down and refuses to move while you are on the road, what is your first priority?

**2.** You are waiting in a stream of traffic at the traffic lights and the lights turn green. However, the car in front of you does not move. Drivers behind you are getting impatient and they start sounding their car horns. You join in. What is wrong with this sequence of events according to the Highway Code?

**3.** In the event of a breakdown, how far away from your vehicle should you place your reflecting, red triangle warning sign. (You are on an *ordinary* road, not a motorway.)

a] 30 yards.          c] 100 feet.
b] 100 yards.         d] 50 yards.

**4.** Because motorway traffic is faster than on ordinary roads and no stopping is allowed in normal circumstances, the reflecting red triangle warning sign must be placed further from a car which has broken down than it needs to be on an ordinary road. Where should the sign be placed?

a] Four times.
b] Six times.
c] Three times the distance required on ordinary roads.

**5.** Your car has broken down at night. As you stand around waiting for the emergency service van to arrive, where should you NOT place yourself?

a] At the rear of your car.
b] Near the kerb.
c] In front of your car.
d] By the side of your car in the road.

**6.** In the event of an accident, what vital information must the police have from a driver or other eyewitness at the scene when being advised of the occurrence?

**7.** In the same circumstances as those in Question 6 above, what must be reported to the ambulance services as a matter of urgent priority?

**8.** There has been an accident involving a vehicle carrying dangerous goods and you are first on the scene. You intend to advise the police and emergency services but, of course, need to let them know the nature of the dangerous goods – be it compressed gas, corrosive substances or toxic materials. This information is displayed on a panel carried by the vehicle. Where should you look for it and what shape will it be?

**9.** A toxic or other dangerous substance falls or leaks from a vehicle travelling on the same road as yourself. What should you do?

**10.** In accidents involving vehicles carrying dangerous goods, why do drivers and others at the scene need to test the direction of the wind when the dangerous goods are liquids and have spilled onto the carriageway?

**11.** If your car breaks down on a motorway, where should you place it, if it is possible to move it?

**12.** The car in front of you has its roof rack loaded with a small boat. Suddenly, a gust of wind rocks the boat and a paddle falls out of it onto the motorway. The driver of the car brakes briefly, as if to stop, then changes his mind and indicates that he is moving left into the next, inner, lane. He parks his car on the hard shoulder and goes to the nearest telephone. The paddle, of course, is still lying on the motorway, a hazard to all traffic that passes by. Has the driver of the car in front done the right thing in leaving it there?

**13.** Name three emergency vehicles which you may see rushing along the road to the scene of an accident.

**14.** While driving along the road, you hear a siren sounding and notice the flash of blue lamps on other vehicles. What kinds of vehicles could these be?

**15.** The signals have indicated that it is safe for you to drive over a level crossing. Just as you reach the centre of it, right between the railway lines, your car stalls and will not re-start. What should you do?

**16.** You have a head cold and are feeling a bit 'woozy'. It is not serious enough for you to go to bed, but you do not want to drive down to the railway station and pick up your mother-in-law, who is arriving for a stay. Your husband (or wife) accuses you of making a fuss and trying to make things difficult for his (or her) mother. Rather than enter into an argument when you are feeling off-colour, you give in and drive to the station. Who is right and who is wrong in such circumstances?

**17.** During a heavy rainstorm, a drain has overflowed and the road is flooded. Also, a tree has been blown over and is lying half across the road. What road sign would you expect to see warning you of dangers like this which lie ahead?

**18.** You are driving through a park, such as Richmond Park in Surrey, when all of a sudden a couple of deer dash across the road in front of you. You are shocked and surprised, but just manage to avoid hitting them. There is a road sign which you have missed seeing, one which would have warned you of this possibility. What is it?

**19.** The car in front of you pulls up suddenly and without warning and although you have allowed a proper distance between yourself and this car, you have to brake hard to avoid running into it. In your fury – and fright – at this incident, you blare your car horn at the offending driver. Are you right to do this?

**20.** You are not allowed to stop on a motorway except when your car breaks down or when you are signalled to stop by police, an emergency traffic sign or a flashing red light signal. There is, however, one other circumstance in which you are allowed to stop on the motorway. What is it?

# Section Eleven
# First Aid on the Road

First Aid in road accidents is something to be undertaken with caution. Unless you are already a trained First Aider, you must take exceptional care in situations which can be as distressing as they are unfamiliar to you. Someone else's life can literally be in your hands and if you genuinely feel unable to cope with the situation it is best to confine yourself to comforting and reassuring accident victims. You can also apply yourself to other non-medical aid. The answers to Questions 2, 3, 4, 5, and 8 will tell you what constitutes this type of aid.

If you shrink from giving First Aid as specified in the Highway Code, please do not consider yourself inadequate. You are not only dealing with an unfamiliar situation, but may yourself be a victim of shock which can impair your ability to take the correct action.

Your best procedure is to prepare yourself for the eventuality which, as stated in the Highway Code, comprises carrying a First Aid Kit (and knowing how to use it) and learning First Aid. Instruction in First Aid is given by the St. John Ambulance Association and Brigade, St. Andrew's Ambulance Association and the British Red Cross Society.

**1.** After an accident, the possibility of further collisions from oncoming traffic is mentioned in the Highway Code as one of two threatened dangers. What is the other?

**2.** After an accident, an ambulance should be called as soon as possible and the ambulance services given information as to the numbers of vehicles and casualties involved. What else is vital for the ambulance services to know?

**3.** Why is a ban on smoking in the area of a road accident an important one?

**4.** Someone at the scene of accident has a thermos flask of tea and wants to give one of the casualties a drink from it. Is this wise?

**5.** A casualty in the passenger seat of a car that has been in an accident asks for help in getting out. Should you or should you not agree?

**6.** What is the first thing you should do for an accident victim whose breathing has stopped?

**7.** After taking the action detailed in the answer to Question 6 above, in which direction should you keep the victim's head tilted as a preliminary to giving mouth-to-mouth resuscitation?

a] Backwards.
b] To one side.
c] Forwards.

**8.** Why should you make sure that an accident victim is not left alone or allowed to become cold?

**9.** You have decided to give mouth-to-mouth resuscitation. What is your first action?

**10.** In mouth-to-mouth resuscitation, how do you know that you efforts are having effect?

**11.** An accident victim has suffered a wound and is bleeding. What should you use to help control the bleeding?

**12.** Through mouth-to-mouth resuscitation, you have managed to get an accident victim breathing. At what intervals should you again apply this method until the casualty can breathe unaided?

# Section Twelve
# Road Junctions and Traffic Lights

**1.** You are about to turn into a road at a road junction and see some pedestrians on the kerb of the former. Should you drive on down the road, after you have turned into it?

**2.** The light signals at a pedestrian crossing show red and amber together, or green, indicating that you may drive on. When should you *NOT* do so, despite what the light signals say?

**3.** What is the difference between traffic signals at Pelican crossings and 'ordinary' traffic lights?

**4.** Can you overtake at a road junction?

**5.** The road on which you are travelling is a local road and you are approaching a main road at the junction ahead. What can you expect to find at the point where your road meets the main road?

**6.** What is the significance of criss cross yellow lines painted on the road?

**7.** What is a box junction?

**8.** At a box junction, you want to turn right. However, the oncoming traffic is too heavy and there are other vehicles waiting to do the same as you. In these circumstances, you may not enter the box. *TRUE* or *FALSE*?

**9.** Are you allowed to let your vehicle wait or park near traffic lights?

**10.** When an amber light shows at the traffic lights, what is it 'telling' you?

**11.** What is the purpose of the green filter arrow which often accompanies sets of traffic lights?

**12.** If you come to a set of traffic lights just as the red and amber lights show together, should you stop or drive on?

**13.** What is the basic difference between traffic lights signalling GO on the ordinary road and at automatic 'open' level crossings?

**14.** The traffic lights at automatic half-barrier level crossings include the sounding of an alarm when signalling traffic to stop. Where, on the ordinary road, do traffic lights also sound alarms?

**15.** A road sign tells you that the traffic lights ahead are not operating. What is on this sign?

**16.** You are waiting at traffic lights at a road junction. The green GO light shows, but vehicles in front of you are at the centre of the junction, queuing up to turn right. Should you move off from the traffic lights?

**17.** A road junction on a three-lane main road has traffic lights with an accompanying filter to the left. Allowing they are in the correct lanes, once the lines had turned green for GO, which direction would traffic in the following positions go?

a] The right-hand lane.
b] The left-hand lane.
c] The middle lane.

**18.** If you see a road sign which shows a road as a straight, upright, black line with a short, red bar across the top, does this mean that there is a 'T' junction ahead?

**19.** A car pulls into the central reservation of a dual carriageway. What is the driver's intention?

**20.** At a set of traffic lights, the main signals show Red and Amber, with a green arrow filter sign also showing to the left. Are you permitted to drive straight on?

**21.** At level crossings, lifting bridges, fire stations and airfields, traffic signals show lights in two colours only. What are these colours?

**22.** Traffic lights on ordinary roads which show the amber light only mean STOP at the stop line, but there are two circumstances in which you may drive on. What are they?

**23.** Name three forms of traffic light signals – single lights or two lights showing together – which mean STOP.

**24.** Name two forms of traffic light signals which mean GO.

**25.** What is the difference between a double, broken white line painted on a road where it meets another at a junction, and a solid white line painted at the same place?

# Section One
# The Road

## A Driver's Tale (1)

One moment the sky overhead seemed clear with little more than a light overcast, the next, David found to his fury that he had driven into a patch of heavy rain. He cursed quietly to himself as he glanced at the sky ahead and saw the grey-black clouds which denoted yet more rain further along the road.

'Just my rotten luck,' David grimaced. 'An important appointment and I'm running late already.' He glanced at his speedometer. It showed forty miles an hour.

David reckoned the grip of his wheels on the road through the feel of his steering wheel.

'Seems okay,' he thought. 'Forty is all right.' Maybe he would be on time after all, or not too late at any rate.

Just then, out of the corner of his left eye, David noticed a car overtaking him. It speeded past, cut smartly in front of David, accelerated a bit and presented him with an infuriating view of its boot and rear window barely thirty yards in front of him.

David cursed again, this time aloud. He felt a tremendous urge to swerve to the right, overtake this fellow and teach him a lesson!

# Questions

**1** What cardinal error – both very dangerous and illegal – was made by the driver of the overtaking car?

**2** What further error did this driver make when moving into the space in front of David's car?

**3** Was the distance between David's car and the overtaking car a safe one in the road conditions then prevailing?

**4** Having been so abruptly overtaken, should David overtake in his turn? If not, what should he do?

# Section Two
# Other Road Users

## A Driver's Tale (2)

'Cheerio, love!' David gave his wife Anne a parting kiss and hugged their three children before getting into his car. He fastened his seat belt, gave a smile and a wave and drove off.

'Lucky old David,' Anne thought, as she watched him go. 'He doesn't have to take the kids to school before going to work, like I do.'

The three children piled into the back of their mother's car. 'Okay, kids,' Anne told them. 'Here we go again.'

Anne started up and headed for the familiar route that led towards the school. She was nearing the junction where, normally, she drove straight on, when ten-year-old Elizabeth piped up: 'Mummy, look! There's a hole in the road and some men working there! Drive past it so we can have a look, please do!'

'Don't be silly, Elizabeth,' Anne told her. 'The road's closed – can't you see the sign. We'll have to make a diversion.'

The diversion made, Anne found herself driving along an unfamiliar road. There seemed to be a lot of pedestrians about. They were going to delay her, Anne thought, feeling flustered and impatient.

Zig zag lines on the road showed her that a Zebra crossing was ahead. She prepared to slow down and, opening her window, made a hand signal to the three pedestrians waiting by the kerb, extending her arm and making circular movement with it.

The pedestrians just stared at her, looking confused. They hovered on the pavement, as if unsure of what to do.

'What's the matter with them?' Anne was becoming annoyed. 'Why won't they cross the road?'

## Questions

**1** Anne and her children omitted something important after getting in their car. What was it?

**2** Apart from signs telling Anne that the road ahead was closed, and the diversion signs, what other warning sign might she have seen?

**3** Where were the zig zag lines indicating a Zebra crossing painted on the road surface?

**4** Why were the pedestrians reluctant to cross at the Zebra crossing after seeing Anne's signal?

# Section Three
# Driving Conditions and Night Driving

## A Driver's Tale (3)

The evening out at the theatre had been very entertaining, and so had the dinner afterwards. Now, David, with Anne beside him in the passenger seat, was enjoying the drive back home through almost empty night-time streets.

Without warning, a cat scampered across the road in front of the car, and instinctively David reacted by sounding the horn.

'You could get had up for that,' Anne teased him.

'No, I can't, David contradicted. 'Look at your watch, my girl!'

Anne did so. 'You sounded that horn with only three minutes to spare, you know. Hey . . .' she said suddenly. 'I just saw three of those street lamps go out. It's pretty murky now.'

David glanced quickly at the lamps. Anne was right. Visibility wasn't all that good now, so he switched his side lights up to dipped headlights.

The car reached the junction where David prepared to turn into the side road that led to the house. Before doing so, he slowed down and looked quickly at the entrance to the side road before driving on.

'You know that road where we saw the cat,' said Anne as David came to a halt in the driveway of their home. 'I counted ten cars parked at my side of the road, and six of them weren't parked properly.'

# Questions

**1** At what time of night did David sound his car horn?

**2** Was David correct to alter his lights from side lights to dipped headlights?

**3** Why did David make a point of scrutinising the entrance to the side road before driving down it?

**4** What told Anne that six out of the ten parked cars were not parked correctly?

# Answers – Section One The Road

**1.** No closer than the overall shortest stopping distance (i.e. thinking *AND* braking distance added together) relative to your car's speed – and then only in good road conditions.

**2.** You must now reckon the safe gap between yourself and the vehicle in front as being between *YOU* and the car which has just overtaken you. You should therefore drop back so that the gap is the proper, safe one.

**3.** No more than the distance which is within the range of your vision. At that distance, other cars, pedestrians and other features should be at least identifiable.

**4.** a] 240 feet.
  b] 120 feet.
  c] 75 feet.

**5.** a] 70 feet.
  b] 50 feet.
  c] 30 feet.

**6.** 80 feet.

**7.** The stopping distance of 40 feet is equally divided – 20 feet for *THINKING*, 20 feet for *BRAKING*.

**8.** Give way to the bus.

**9.** When driving in fog, it is vital to slow down to a safe speed. In addition, you should watch your speed indicator in order to check that you are not accelerating without being aware of it. It is, in any case, wise to check your speedometer occasionally even when driving in normal conditions. This habit, once established, makes it easier to make the checks when it is particularly important to do so.

**10.** Cyclists on the road have a 'narrow' profile. They are therefore less easy for motorists and other road users to see. In the case of *pedal* cyclists, they are also slower than other road users.

**11.** Sleepiness can be kept at bay by ensuring there is a good supply of fresh air in the car. Open both the passenger and driving-side front windows.

**12.** At 40 mph.

**13.** Do *not* speed up, since this will shorten the safe distance between yourself and the car in front of you. However, keep as far in front as you can.

**14.** Reckon at least 2 yards for every mile per hour of your driving speed.

**15.** When road signs or markings indicate that right-hand driving is allowed. You may also keep to the right-hand side of the road when you intend to overtake or to turn right, and in addition, when you pass stationary vehicles or pedestrians on the road, as long as it is safe for you to do so.

**16.** Move out a sufficient distance to the right to keep your car well clear of the vehicles and pedestrians.

**17.** Policemen, traffic wardens, and officials in charge of school road-crossing patrols.

**18.** Loads carried on or towed by vehicles must be securely tied or fastened to minimise the danger of falling off or of spilling onto the road while you are driving.

**19.** Two lanes are open, i.e. those lanes running beneath the arrows.

**20.** There are five exits/entrances on this roundabout – the four indicated by the green direction sign and the road on which you are travelling.

**21.** 'Ring Road.'

**22.** By white arrows painted on the road surface.

**23.** That there is a sharp bend in the road just ahead. If the road is about to bend sharply to the *LEFT*, the white chevrons will point to the left. It is advisable, if safe, to slow down on seeing the 'sharp bend' sign, since too much speed may pull your car out into the opposite lane as you round the corner.

**24.** a] Stop at the stop line, but only if you are *NOT* already across the line, or if, by pulling up, you could cause an accident.

b] Stop. However, be aware that the green GO signal will follow quite soon.

c] Stop if you are going to drive straight on, but GO if you are following the filter signal and turning left.

**25.** When signalled to stop by a police officer or an emergency traffic sign, or by a flashing red light signal.

**26.** The deceleration lane on a motorway is the extra lane which allows you to slow down safely before entering the exit slip road. There, and in the ordinary road beyond, traffic conditions and speed will be quite different from those obtaining on the motorway. The deceleration or 'slowing down' lane is somewhat like the de-pressurisation chamber which deep sea divers have to enter in order to normalise before return to surface pressure above.

**27.** You must leave the motorway at the next exit, because of an accident or some other obstruction ahead.

**28.** When normal conditions prevail on the motorway, the special signs are completely blank.

**29.** Flashing amber signals indicate danger in some form. This might be an obstruction due to an accident, slippery road surfaces ahead which could cause skidding, or perhaps a patch of fog of which you are unaware.

**30.** *FALSE*! *NEVER EVER* retrieve a fallen object from the motorway yourself. Instead, leave it and watch out for the nearest roadside telephone, from which you can telephone and inform the police of what has happened *and* where it has occurred.

**31.** In no circumstances whatsoever. You may never switch on your hazard warning lights while driving along a road, only in appropriate circumstances when your car is stationary, such as after a breakdown.

**32.** a] At least 50 yards from your car.
b] At least 150 yards from your car.

# Answers –
# Section Two
# Other Road Users

**1.** Motor vehicles over 7,500 kgs maximum gross weight and trailers over 3,500 kgs maximum gross weight.

**2.** Rectangular boards painted in red and yellow slanted stripes.

**3.** One signal indicator light at a time, either to your left or your right, depending on which move or turn you wish to make.

**4.** Having wound down the driver's window, extend your arm and make a circular movement with it.

**5.** You extend your arm from the driver's window and move it up and down.

**6.** a] Indicates the point at which you should give way to traffic from the right at *a 'mini' roundabout.*

b] Indicates the point at which you should give way to traffic from the right on a *roundabout.*

c] Indicates the point where you must give way to traffic on a *major road.*

**7.** The sign shows a single-decker bus with a direction arrow and, beneath it, the words BUS LANE.

**8.** The other feature is the rear end of a car towing the caravan.

**9.** A rectangular panel with a light blue background and a pedal cycle illustrated in white.

**10.** You should make a habit of glancing in your rear-view driving mirror *regularly* in order to see who is behind you and what they are doing. The overall purpose is to get a picture of the road to the rear of your car.

**11.** Glance behind and look in the mirror.

**12.** You must look in your rear-view mirror to check traffic behind you.

**13.** Calculate 1 yard for every mile per hour of your speed.

**14.** Ambulances. Fire engines. Police vehicles.

**15.** a] and d] YES.
　　b] c] and e] NO.

**16.** To move back into the left-hand lane as soon as possible and as safely as possible.

**17.** In all cases, an emergency vehicle is approaching.

**18.** The led horse should be on the left of the rider so that the latter is between the former and the traffic on the road.

**19.** At road bends or on the brow of a hill, herds of animals cannot be seen in advance by oncoming drivers. When driving in the countryside, near farmland, and particularly in summer, it is therefore wise to approach road bends and the brows of hills with great care.

**20.** a] b] c] and e] are *NOT* permitted to use motorways.
As for d] Motorcyclists – only large motorcycles may use motorways.

**21.** No. It is an offence to pick up hitchhikers on slip roads and also on the motorways to which they lead. In any case, as a pedestrian, the hitchhiker has no right to be on a motorway in the first place.

**22.** A herd of animals is being driven or ridden along the road. The white front and red back lights indicate the size of the herd and the amount of room it occupies on the road.

**23.** The driver is loading or unloading.

**24.** Check that pedestrians, cyclists and other vehicles on the road are not so near that they will collide with your open door.

**25.** a] NO. Use full headlights.

b] NO. Use side lights only.

c] YES.

d] YES.

**26.** If you wish another road user to be aware of your presence.

**27.** If you wish to warn other road users of your presence.

**28.** NO. You should wait until it *actually* turns left before you drive on. Never ASSUME the signal is correct. Wait and make sure first.

**29.** On the right.

**30.** Pedestrians on the pavement *AND* traffic using the road.

**31.** A Zebra crossing provides a specified and visible crossing place for pedestrians to traverse the road.

**32.** When pedestrians want to cross the road other than at a place specified for this (such as a Zebra crossing) you should not signal them to cross because, although you may be willing to stop for them, you cannot know whether other approaching vehicles will do the same.

**33.** A Zebra crossing.

**34.** Pedestrian crossings may be controlled by police officers, by traffic wardens, or by sets of lights.

**35.** When a *straight* Pelican crossing has a central refuge it is *ONE* crossing.

**36.** STOP ... CHILDREN.

**37.** The location of the accident and details of any casualties.

**38.** *NO*. Stop if you see the barrier descending or the level crossing gates starting to close – whether or not the red STOP lights are showing.

**39.** Holidaymakers, probably with cars loaded with luggage. HR means 'Holiday Route.'

**40.** a] A picture of flames in black and white.

b] An 'O' with flames on top, in black.

c] A gas cylinder, in black.

d] Three triangles, with points arranged around a central black dot.

e] Test tubes pouring drops onto a black bar-shaped object and hand, and corroding or destroying them.

**41.** a] and d] = iii]

b] = ii]

c] = iv]

e] = i]

f] = v]

**42.** A triangle with white and red slanted stripes.

**43.** Because the vehicle is longer than others on the road, it will need longer to overtake. Extra care must therefore be taken to ensure that other traffic on the road and also the road conditions allow enough time for this more prolonged manoeuvre.

# Answers – Section Three Driving Conditions and Night Driving

**1.** The word FORD.

**2.** a] No.

b] Yes.

c] Yes, but only because the pedestrian is crossing the road.

d] Yes.

e] Yes, but not during prohibited times.

f] Yes.

g] Yes. The times you may *NOT* park at a bus stop are 7 a.m. to 7 p.m.

**3.** a] You may sound your horn if you have to up to 11.30 p.m. but not afterwards.

b] No.

c] Yes.

d] *No.*

**4.** 60 miles per hour.

**5.** b] At least doubled, but this is a minimum. The greater the distance between yourself and the car in front commensurate with other road safety factors, the better.

**6.** Outside the times during which the buses use the lane. However, some bus lanes are in operation for the whole 24 hours and so may never be used by other vehicles.

**7.** In conditions of fog or mist or at night or dusk it can be more difficult to judge speed and distance than it is during the daytime.

**8.** No. Stay where you are and be patient.

**9.** You should watch out for pedestrians crossing the road into which you are turning. You must be prepared to give way to them.

**10.** That normal conditions prevail on the motorway.

**11.** The amber lights flash.

**12.** That there is a sharp bend to the left in the road ahead.

**13.** An exclamation mark means that there is a danger unspecified by another sign lying ahead. There may, for example, be a flood in the road due to a blocked drain, or a tree could have fallen across the road. Sometimes, the sign with the exclamation mark may be accompanied by another sign detailing the danger in words.

**14.** Two pairs of alternating flashing red lights.

**15.** Keep on driving!

**16.** Wait at the side until both halves of the dual carriageway are clear enough for you to turn into it in one continuous movement.

**17.** You should avoid doing anything that will unduly frighten the animals, such as driving by too fast, sounding your horn or 'revving' your engine.

**18.** It is a hazard warning sign.

**19.** By telephoning the signalman, using the special railway telephone provided. If it is safe to cross, do so as quickly as possible, then telephone the signalman again to advise that you have done so.

**20.** By looking both ways and listening.

**21.** Fifteen yards.

**22.** Standing behind the rear of your vehicle when it has broken down at night could obscure the rear lamps. This may provide a potential hazard to other traffic on the road.

**23.** Another train is approaching.

**24.** a] *Facing* the direction of the traffic.

**25.** You should give the emergency services details of the labels and markings on the side of the vehicle. These indicate the nature of the dangerous contents.

**26.** The pedestrian is both deaf and blind.

**27.** People under 15 and over 60 may not be able to judge speeds well and, in misjudging the speed of your oncoming car, could step out into the road unexpectedly.

**28.** To slow down to a safe speed and watch your speed indicator to see you are not accelerating without being aware that you are doing so.

**29.** In wet or slippery road conditions.

**30.** *No.* Resist the urge to speed up, but keep as far in front of the vehicle behind you as you safely can.

**31.** The short red bar across a line indicating a route shows that the route is closed.

**32.** Because other road users could experience difficultly in seeing the road clearly.

**33.** a] Yes.

b] Yes.

c] No. Headlamps should be used where the street lights are more than *200 yards* apart.

d] Yes.

e] No. Seriously reduced visibility is reckoned at less than *100 metres*.

**34.** You are not allowed to wear tinted spectacles at night nor in conditions of poor visibility, since they restrict your vision and this could be dangerous.

**35.** The first sign indicates that the road narrows on the right only. The second sign shows that it narrows on both sides.

**36.** A triangular red-edged sign showing a deer in silhouette.

# Answers – Section Four Motorways, Primary Routes and Local Roads

## Motorways

**1.** The sign shows a two-lane road with a bridge over it in white.

**2.** Motorway signs have light blue backgrounds. Primary route signs have green backgrounds. The most common local road signs have white backgrounds.

**3.** It means that the M1 can be reached from the M10 at a point further along the M10.

**4.** *FALSE*, in both cases.

**5.** There is no such thing as the 'fast' lane on the motorway. There are only driving lane and overtaking lanes.

**6.** a] = ii].
b] = i].
c] = iii].

**7.** No, you cannot reverse your car on a motorway.

**8.** *TRUE*, in both cases.

**9.** On the hard shoulder.

**10.** On the left-hand side.

**11.** A lighted arrow indicating a turn to the left.

**12.** Because speeds on motorways can seem slower than they really are. The Highway Code cites one example:

50 mph can seem like 30 mph, because other traffic on the motorway may be moving faster than you are and so can give you no reference from which you are able to reckon your own speed accurately.

**13.** First, look to see if there is a telephone immediately in sight. If not, look at the signs on marker posts which will show you the direction of the nearest telephone.

**14.** Each white bar represents 100 yards.

**15.** That you should change lanes.

# Primary Routes and Local Roads

**1.** Short, white, widely-spaced bars.

**2.** You *DON'T* move it. You extend your arm and hold it there.

**3.** That you are slowing down or intend to stop.

**4.** You are telling the police officer that you want to drive straight on.

**5.** STOP!

**6.** c] Local direction signs have light blue borders.

**7.** Yes, but only if there is room for you to clear the junction safely. If it is not safe, then you will have to wait and if the lights again turn red while you are waiting, you will have to start the process again.

**8.** In the centre or in the right-hand lane.

**9.** To your right. Your car and the other car should be offside to offside.

**10.** In the central reservation.

**11.** a] No.

b] Yes, but *ONLY* where traffic may pass on either side.

c] Yes, but only in order to turn left or to park.

d] Yes.

**12.** 'Ring Road.'

**13.** The green GO signal will shortly follow the red/amber signal, sometimes thought of as the 'Get Ready' signal.

**14.** They are both GIVE WAY signs. The seven-sided sign means STOP *and* GIVE WAY. The triangular sign means GIVE WAY TO TRAFFIC ON MAJOR ROAD AHEAD.

**15.** You signal your intention to leave the roundabout as you are passing the *SECOND* exit, i.e. the exit before yours. Use the left turn indicator when passing the second exit.

**16.** Definitely not!

**17.** To warn, help or inform other road users and therefore contribute to safe use of the roads.

**18.** Pull in at the first opportunity (possibly at a passing place or layby) and allow the faster vehicle to overtake.

**19.** Yes, in all cases, but only where there is a serious reduction in visibility i.e. to less than 100 metres.

**20.** You should undo your seat belt. The wearing of seat belts in cars is now obligatory for drivers and front seat passengers, but there are exceptions and a driver making a reversing manoeuvre is one of them.

**21.** The lights *go out.*

**22.** An automatic half-barrier level crossing is a crossing at a railway lane with an automatic barrier across the left-hand side of the road only. Other level crossings may have barriers or gates across *BOTH* sides of the road. The half-barrier is a horizontal plank painted in red and white stripes.

**23.** Stop opposite the passing place so that the oncoming vehicle may use it.

**24.** Vehicles in the main road have the right of way.

**25.** For overtaking or for turning right.

**26.** When there are slower vehicles in the left-hand lane. However, once you have passed them, you should yourself return to the left-hand lane.

**27.** By moving, in good time, to the correct lane for your exit.

**28.** a] and c] *No!*
b] and d] Yes.

**29.** The middle lane, in both cases.

# Answers –
# Section Five
# You and Your Car

**1.** By half.

**2.** At the age of fourteen.

**3.** Light-coloured, or reflective and fluorescent clothing.

**4.** Well-behaved or not, you should never let your dog out of your car without first attaching a lead.

**5.** In the rear seat, wearing an approved, properly fitted child safety harness.

**6.** You can leave the L-plates as fitted as long as you cover them up. Otherwise, remove them.

**7.** The driver and the front-seat passenger.

**8.** No. Reversing is one of the exceptions to the law requiring drivers to wear seat belts, because it can restrict your ability to see properly out of the back of the car.

**9.** That it be suitable for the child's age and weight (or size).

**10.** The fitting of child safety locks which should always be checked before starting a journey.

**11.** By flashing your lights or sounding your car horn.

**12.** When you are feeling tired or are unwell, even if it's only a slight cold.

**13.** Improperly adjusted headlamps can dazzle the driver of an oncoming car and cause an accident.

**14.** A small rectangular sign with a yellow background and black edging which says HR in black capital letters.

**15.** The police officer is telling you to move out from the side.

**16.** That you mean to move or turn left.

**17.** That you mean to move or turn right.

**18.** By showing him the palm of your upraised left hand.

**19.** Have a break. Pull in at the first suitable parking place or layby and rest for a while until you feel more refreshed.

**20.** You have forgotten to make the appropriate signal i.e. use your direction light indicator.

**21.** Lock it.

**22.** Spare tyre and windscreen wipers.

**23.** So that they do not fall off in the road while you are driving and cause a potentially dangerous obstruction to traffic.

**24.** Your hazard warning lights.

**25.** You must not open the door, but should wait until the cyclist has gone past.

**26.** The hazard warning device is a switch which allows all your direction indicators to flash simultaneously.

**27.** You did not place the reflecting triangle far enough away from your car. On an ordinary road, a distance of 50 yards is sufficient. On the motorway, this should be trebled, to 150 yards.

**28.** Windscreen wipers. Headlamps or front fog lamps.

**29.** 45 yards.

**30.** You may be able to see round a bend in the road when it goes right because you are viewing it from the left-hand side of the road. A left bend in the road is, however, largely concealed from your forward vision.

# Answers – Section Six Markings on the Road

**1.** A rectangular space enclosed in broken white lines with BUS STOP written inside.

**2.** By white arrows painted on the road surface.

**3.** The entrance to a side road.

**4.** School.

**5.** A 'mini' roundabout.

**6.** The stop line at the STOP sign is broader.

**7.** a] Three yellow lines.

b] One line.

c] Two lines.

**8.** Short, white, widely-spaced bars.

**9.** A single line of long, white rectangles spaced their own width apart.

**10.** Yellow lines painted *ON THE ROAD* indicate waiting restrictions. Yellow lines painted *ON THE KERB* indicate loading and unloading restrictions.

**11.** The double yellow line.

**12.** Long, white rectangles, spaced their own length apart.

**13.** A point at which you must give way to other traffic.

**14.** See Question 13 in this section!

**15.** a] Yes.

b] No.

c] Yes.

**16.** a] No.

b] Yes.

c] Yes.

d] No.

**17.** You may cross the broken white line when overtaking as long as it is safe to do so. In addition, you must be able to complete your overtaking, that is return safely to the left hand driving lane, *BEFORE* the start of double white lines on the road which have the solid line nearer to you.

**18.** Zig zag lines on either side of the driving lane.

**19.** a] Amber studs indicate the central reservation of dual carriageways.

b] Red studs mark the edge of the carriageway on the left-hand side.

c] White studs are often used in conjunction with white lines to indicate the centre of a road, or to mark the road lanes.

d] Green studs are used to indicate laybys and side roads.

**20.** Definitely not. Overtaking is a manoeuvre which you should *NEVER* make once you know a Zebra crossing is ahead.

**21.** No. If pedestrians are waiting on the kerb to cross a Zebra crossing, you must wait for them to do so.

**22.** Green studs on a motorway indicate the line separating the acceleration and deceleration lanes from the through carriageway.

**23.** Red studs on a motorway indicate the left-hand edge of the carriageway.

**24.** Yes, but *only* in an emergency, such as a manoeuvre that will avoid an accident.

**25.** White lines and white studs together may mark the centre of the road or driving lanes on the road.

# Answers –
# Section Seven
# Signs on the Road

**1.** Triangular.

**2.** No pedestrians.

**3.** The arrows, one above the other, point right (top) and left (bottom).

**4.** The light signals have failed.

**5.** No overtaking. The sign implies that the red car – red because it is in a dangerous position in a 'no overtaking' situation – is the overtaking car.

**6.** A diamond-shaped sign, white at the top and red at the bottom. The white part shows black and white 'flames' and the lower part, the words SPONTANEOUSLY COMBUSTIBLE. 'Spontaneously combustible' means that the material is volatile and can burst into flames or burn on its own.

**7.** a] is carried on the side of the vehicle b] at the rear.

**8.** At airfields, lifting bridges, level crossings or fire stations.

**9.** These signs give orders and are mostly prohibitive.

**10.** The sign indicates a route which is shared by pedal cyclists and pedestrians.

**11.** The first sign means that 30 mph is the minimum speed. The second indicates that this speed limit no longer applies. These signs are often found on roads in built-up areas, especially where there are shops.

**12.** '... PHONE AND GET PERMISSION TO CROSS.'

**13.** 5 mph or less.

**14.** Three. The top sign shows two humps in a white, red-edged, triangular panel.

**15.** a] Two arrows pointing to the bottom right and left of the circle mean that vehicles may pass on either side.

b] Three arrows round the edge of a blue circular sign are found at 'mini' roundabouts. This means, by inference, that you must give way to vehicles coming from the immediate right.

**16.** The sign with the gate indicates a level crossing with a barrier or gate. The sign with the steam engine indicates that the level crossing ahead has *NO* barrier or gate.

**17.** The sign indicates low flying aircraft in the vicinity – possibly from a local flying club – or that there may be sudden aircraft noise which could startle you. The sign is a white, red-edged, upright triangle.

**18.** The signs are white with black borders and black printing.

**19.** A white, black-edged sign showing the letter 'R'.

**20.** The sign indicates a diversion route.

**21.** The arrows tell you to GET IN LANE for the destinations shown on another, blue, panel above the black one.

**22.** The sign means that *CARS* are not allowed. However, solo motorcycles, scooters and mopeds *are* allowed to use the road.

**23.** An exclamation mark in black is shown on a triangular, white, red-edged sign.

**24.** That there are wild animals in the vicinity. There are, however, other signs indicating the presence of specific wild animals, such as badgers or frogs and toads.

**25.** Light blue.

**26.** The road on which you are travelling goes straight on, with another road leading off to the left.

**27.** *TRUE.*

**28.** The sign is in two parts. The larger, upper part contains a light blue circle edged in red, with a red diagonal and the words METER ZONE beneath. The lower, smaller panel indicates the periods at which the meters can be used.

**29.** The sign and signals indicate a place of particular danger, requiring very careful driving.

**30.** Two white, downward-pointing arrows above the lanes which are open. Two red 'X's above the lanes which are closed. The use of red, of course, infers danger if you were unwise enough to try to proceed along the 'closed' lanes.

**31.** The sign is a white rectangle which shows, in black, the rear end of a car towing a caravan.

**32.** The sign indicates a hospital nearby. The word 'hospital' is, in fact, written under the 'H' on the sign.

**33.** 200 yards.

**34.** The sign denotes NO THROUGH ROAD.

**35.** A panel with alternating flashing amber lights. In the centre panel, the left and the centre lanes are shown as straight vertical lines. The right-hand lane, however, shows as a vertical line with two horizontal bars across the top. All the lanes on this sign are indicated by means of lines of lights.

**36.** A square of lights with cut off corners. A diagonal bar of lights runs from the top right to the lower left-hand corner.

**37.** Move into another lane. The lane with the red light signal is closed, and you should not proceed beyond the signal.

**38.** The approach of a train, soon to arrive on the level crossing.

**39.** Do not move further along this lane.

**40.** PERMIT HOLDERS ONLY, meaning that parking is restricted to those holding permits to park there, for instance residents.

**41.** The long, black, horizontal sign will show a line of white chevrons pointing to the left.

**42.** '... LIGHTS SHOW.'

**43.** Neither. Both lines of traffic have equal priority.

**44.** This sign indicates that there is more than one railway line using the level crossing.

**45.** A white, red-edged triangle with a broken black circle in the centre.

**46.** Signs showing silhouettes of people could feature two elderly folk; an adult and a child, showing that there are pedestrians on the road ahead; a man walking, indicating a pedestrian crossing ahead; two children running, showing the presence nearby of a school.

**47.** That the road ahead is about to narrow on both sides.

**48.** The round blue sign which has a smaller arrow means AHEAD ONLY. The rectangular blue sign, which has a larger arrow, means ONE-WAY TRAFFIC.

# Answers –
# Section Eight
# Roundabouts and Level Crossings

**1.** The basic purpose of a roundabout is to keep traffic moving at a good pace. Without roundabouts, particularly at very busy road junctions, the traffic could easily become jammed.

**2.** A 'mini' roundabout is, as its name suggests, small in size. It may be just a small white hump in the road, or simply a painted circle. Mini roundabouts are often found at smaller road junctions which carry a lot of traffic.

**3.** Mini roundabouts surrounding a larger roundabout also have the basic purpose of keeping traffic moving. If the main roundabout is very large and has numerous exits, traffic could become jammed on it. The mini roundabouts, where roundabout driving rules apply individually, assist traffic in reaching the desired exit more easily. It is therefore possible to find traffic on a 'main roundabout plus mini roundabouts' system moving in either direction.

**4.** Traffic already on a roundabout or mini roundabout has the right of way and vehicles on approach roads must give way.

**5.** On reaching a roundabout, the first thing you must do is assess the traffic on it, if any. If traffic is moving towards you from the right, you must give way to it. However, if the roundabout is clear, keep moving.

**6.** There are no roundabouts on motorways – or traffic lights, pedestrians, scooters or cyclists! Or, indeed, any other feature of ordinary roads which may oblige you to stop or slow down.

**7.** b] Right to left.

**8.** Yes – you have signalled correctly.

**9.** a] When turning left.

b] When turning right.

**10.** An 'open' level crossing is one in which the crossing is not separated from the traversing road by gates or barriers.

**11.** No. The flashing red STOP lights indicate that a second train is approaching the level crossing.

**12.** That it is safe to go over the level crossing.

**13.** An automatic barrier level crossing which is operated by a train as it passes a certain point before reaching the crossing. At such crossings, the half-barriers descend just before the train reaches them.

**14.** The crossings described in the question are 'open' level crossings and the sign there says GIVE WAY or STOP.

**15.** Between the showing of the amber and the red STOP light an alarm sounds.

**16.** Stop! A train will reach the level crossing shortly.

**17.** The half-barrier at an automatic level crossing has red and white horizontal stripes.

**18.** A level crossing without barrier or gate.

**19.** a] One railway line is indicated by the main diagonal cross.

b] If there is more than one line, the bottom half of the diagonal cross is reproduced below it.

**20.** ... LIGHTS SHOW.

**21.** A white, red-edged triangle with a broken black circle in the centre.

**22.** A level crossing with a barrier or gate.

**23.** There will be a picture of a gate on a triangular red-edged sign.

**24.** Below the red-edged, white cross, there is a triangular, white GIVE WAY sign edged in red. Below that, there is a panel edged in black containing the silhouette of a steam engine.

**25.** The sign described in the question can also be seen near airfields, fire stations and lifting bridges.

**26.** a] No.

b] Definitely not.

c] Yes, driving on is the right thing to do and as quickly as safety will allow.

**27.** Yes. Use the clearest convenient lane on your approach to the roundabout and follow it through the roundabout. 'Convenient' in this context means the lane most relevant to the exit from the roundabout which you wish to take.

**28.** The lane which follows through from the lane by which you originally approached the roundabout.

**29.** No. Traffic moves clockwise on a roundabout in Britain and other countries which drive on the left-hand side of the road.

**30.** You signal a left turn and operate it on entering the roundabout from the approach lane.

**31.** Normally, the lane in which you approach the roundabout depends on whether you wish to turn right or left or to go forward when leaving the roundabout. Approach in the left-hand lane when turning left or going forward; approach in the right-hand lane when turning right.

**32.** When turning right onto a roundabout, signal with your right-hand indicator. Keep the indicator operating until you reach the exit before the one you wish to take. At that juncture, change to the left-hand indicator.

**33.** A red light.

**34.** Look up the track and down the track to check whether you can see a train on the line. Looking both ways like this, as well as listening for the sound of an approaching train should needless to say be done from the *edge* of the railway line.

**35.** An automatic half-barrier level crossing.

**36.** Drivers of large and/or slow-moving vehicles must telephone the line signalman, using the special railway telephone provided. Being able to view the state of the track further away from the level crossing, the signalman can tell the driver if it is safe to cross. Once over the crossing, the driver must telephone back to the signalman to inform him of this fact.

**37.** c] 5 mph or less.

**38.** The two humps on the sign indicate a level crossing where the ground clearance is low and, consequently, special care should be taken.

**39.** Level crossings do not have the 'Red–Amber–Green' lights found on ordinary roads. They have their own special system of signals.

**40.** First of all, watch out for vehicles crossing or about to cross in front of your own, and give way to them.

# Answers –
# Section Nine
# Parking and Waiting

**1.** *NO.* You should wait until the oncoming vehicle has passed before moving out a sufficient distance to the right in order to pass the parked vehicle.

**2.** The colour of a Disabled Person's badge is orange and it is displayed on the windscreen.

**3.** Watch out for pedestrians, especially children. Preoccupied with their purchase at the mobile shop or with the book they have just borrowed from the library, they may wander out into the road unexpectedly.

**4.** You are not allowed to park your car on the motorway, except in case of a breakdown or accident, when you may park on the hard shoulder.

**5.** The same answer as Question 4 above also applies here.

**6.** You need to move out a sufficient distance to the right, but must not do so unless it is safe.

**7.** No.

**8.** A fire hydrant affords the water supply which may have to be used by the fire brigade in the event of a blaze nearby. A hydrant consists of a short, stocky pillar usually sited on the pavement near the kerb.

**9.** The brow of a hill, where a parked car could not be seen by traffic coming in the opposite direction until the very last moment.

**10.** All the entrances mentioned may be used by emergency vehicles, such as ambulances or fire engines.

**11.** Because parking opposite a traffic island would unduly narrow the road and restrict the movement of vehicles along the road.

**12.** The hazard warning lights on the car will be flashing.

**13.** You must check that there are no cyclists or other vehicles close behind which may run into the open door of your car - and you.

**14.** b] Two vehicles.

**15.** You must pull up your handbrake firmly.

**16.** c] 30 mph or less.

**17.** c] 15 yards.

**18.** You should give way and allow the bus to proceed.

**19.** a] No.

b] Yes, but only if absolutely necessary.

c] Yes, but not during prohibited times.

d] Yes. The times when you may not park at a bus stop are 7 a.m. to 7 p.m.

**20.** a] Yes, but only because the pedestrian is crossing the road, not at any other time.

b] Yes, but only if absolutely necessary.

c] Yes.

**21.** You must always have your dog on a lead before it can get out of the car and that applies whether it is well-behaved and obedient or not.

**22.** 'AT ANY TIME.'

**23.** Plates with light blue backgrounds.

**24.** Yellow lines over the kerb indicate restrictions on loading and unloading.

**25.** Along the edge of the road.

**26.** No loading at any time.

**27.** 9.30 a.m. to 4.30 p.m.

**28.** The second sentence in the question should read, in full, as follows:

This indicates no waiting for *AT LEAST EIGHT HOURS* between 7 a.m. and 7 p.m. on *FOUR OR MORE* days of the week.

**29.** Most definitely not!

**30.** Just as definitely not!

**31.** A motorway is, in many senses, a segregated driving area, completely cut off, except through its slip road entrances and exits, from the wider road system. In this context, a motorway services area provides motorway travellers with the facilities you would find on an ordinary road – shops, food, petrol, parking and even one-arm bandits and amusement arcades. These services are situated in an area well away from the actual motorway and apart from providing motorway travellers with supplies and victualling, it also gives a chance for them to rest and relax during what can be a long, tense and often tedious journey.

**32.** Special parking facilities may be provided for residents in a parking meter area, or for doctors who have no time to waste looking for a place to park.

**33.** A Disc Zone, which is indicated by signs on the road, is a street or square where drivers have made special applications to park there. Their vehicles are identified by a disc displayed, normally, on the windscreen. Cars parked in Disc Zones which do not have these discs are illegally parked.

**34.** You should *never* wait at or near a level crossing. Nor should you park there, of course.

**35.** No. A pavement is for pedestrians and not vehicles, no matter how wide it may be.

**36.** Laybys.

**37.** No, you cannot.

**38.** *FALSE.*

**39.** As near to the kerb as possible without damaging or scraping your tyres.

**40.** Parking in
[b] a tunnel or
[d] a passing place on a single-track road
would hold up traffic. Parking next to [a] a fire hydrant or at [c] a doctor's premises could block places used by emergency vehicles.

# Answers –
# Section Ten
# Breakdowns, Accidents
# and Mishaps

**1.** Your first priority is to move your car to the side of the road, out of the way of traffic. If necessary, ask passers-by to help you push your vehicle to a safe place.

**2.** According to the Highway Code, you should sound your car horn *ONLY* to make other drivers aware of your presence in the course of driving. In the sequence described in Question 2 you and the drivers behind the non-moving car are sounding car horns out of frustration and annoyance. In addition, none of you is having much consideration for the driver of the non-moving car. He or she may be in some sort of trouble, either with the car or because of suddenly feeling ill. Help the driver if you can. The next time, it may be you.

**3.** On an ordinary road, the reflecting, red triangle warning sign indicating a breakdown should be placed [d] 50 yards from your car.

**4.** On a motorway, the triangle warning sign should be placed 150 yards from the car, that is [c] three times the distance required on ordinary roads.

**5.** You should not stand [a] at the rear of your car because other drivers may not see your rear lights and will be unaware of your presence. You should not place yourself, either, [c] on the road side of your car because you could be hit by oncoming cars.

**6.** The location of the accident.

**7.** The number of casualties and as many details about their injuries as you can possibly give them with reasonable accuracy. Don't exaggerate – that won't help anybody.

**8.** The information panel is placed on the back or side of the vehicle and it is a diamond-shape.

**9.** Keep well away from the spillage and inform the police or the fire brigade.

**10.** Dangerous liquids spilled on the roadway may give off vapours or may contaminate dust lying on the road. While it is always advisable to keep well away from the vehicle concerned, the wind may carry vapours or dust towards you. It is therefore wise to test the direction of the wind in order to know where to position yourself more safely.

**11.** On the hard shoulder.

**12.** Yes, the driver in this question has done the right thing. The alternative – stopping his car and getting out to retrieve the paddle – would be far more dangerous both to himself and other traffic. It is, in any case, banned in the Highway Code. The driver is also correct in pulling over onto the hard shoulder, which can be used in emergency, and in telephoning the police.

**13.** Fire engines. Ambulances. Police vehicles.

**14.** Emergency vehicles, as detailed in the Answer to Question 13 above.

**15.** Get out of the car *immediately* and get off the railway line to a safe place. It is better to lose your car than your life. If possible, inform the signalman or other authority of what has occurred. You could, for instance, use the telephone provided at level crossings.

**16.** Both of you are wrong. Your first thought – not to drive to the station – was the correct one. Drivers should not undertake journeys, however short or local, when they are not feeling well, since this can impair their reactions and judgement on the road. The spouse – whether husband or wife – is wrong to pressurise the driver into going by car and while giving in is understandable in such circumstances, it is better to stick to the first resolve – not to go.

**17.** The road sign which warns of miscellaneous dangers lying ahead in the road (any of which could cause accidents) is a white, red-edged triangle containing a large exclamation mark in black.

**18.** The sign which you missed seeing is the one which indicates the presence of wild animals in an area by the road. This consists of a white, red-edged triangle showing the silhouette of a deer.

**19.** No matter what the provocation, you should not sound your car horn in anger or reproach, only to let drivers know of your presence while in the normal course of using the road.

**20.** You may stop on the motorway if, by doing so, you will avoid an accident.

# Answers –
# Section Eleven
# First Aid on the Road

**1.** The second threatened danger is *FIRE*, perhaps from spilled petrol or other inflammable liquid or from a fractured petrol tank.

**2.** The location of the accident.

**3.** Apart from the inadvisability of smoking in the presence of injured people, there is the fire hazard mentioned in the answer to Question 1 above.

**4.** It is most definitely *NOT* wise. Accident victims should never be given anything to drink. They may have internal injuries which might worsen if they drink.

**5.** However hard it may be to refuse, casualties should not be moved unless there is the threat of danger from further collisions or from fire. Accident victims with back injuries may become paralysed if inexpertly moved and further damage could be inflicted to broken limbs.

**6.** Clear the mouth of obvious obstructions, such as false teeth.

**7.** a] Backwards, that is, as far back as possible. This is done in order to clear the victim's airway.

**8.** Apart from the comfort which the presence of another person may give accident victims, they should not be left alone in case their condition suddenly gets worse, e.g. they stop breathing and become unconscious. The person who is with them can then give mouth-to-mouth resuscitation and may thereby save their lives. Accident victims should not be allowed to get cold because this will increase their discomfort and may also make their condition deteriorate.

**9.** Pinch the casualty's nostrils together so that the air blown into the mouth will reach the lungs.

**10.** When the victim's chest starts to rise.

**11.** A clean pad of material applied to the wound with firm hand pressure. Take care, though, not to press on a foreign body in the wound, such as splinters of glass or pieces of metal, as this will make the wound worse and cause the victim extra pain.

**12.** Four seconds.

# Answers –
# Section Twelve
# Road Junctions and
# Traffic Lights

**1.** No, you should always be prepared to give way to pedestrians in such situations.

**2.** While pedestrians are still crossing the road in front of you.

**3.** 'Ordinary' traffic lights are automatically controlled. Traffic lights at a Pelican crossing may be operated by pedestrians who can change the lights to red for STOP by pressing a button specified for this purpose.

**4.** *NEVER!* This is most dangerous.

**5.** Broken white lines in front of your car, indicating that traffic on the main road has the right of way.

**6.** The criss cross yellow lines form a box junction.

**7.** Criss cross lines painted in yellow at a junction, forming a 'box' which you may not enter unless you can drive straight over it safely.

**8.** No, you may not enter the box unless you can clear it safely and quickly.

**9.** Definitely not. A car parked near traffic lights would constitute an obstruction and could obscure the lights from other drivers.

**10.** Stop at the stop line as long as you are not already across the line or pulling up would cause an accident.

**11.** It allows traffic to turn right or left, whichever the arrow indicates, while traffic driving straight on has to halt. 'Filtering off' the turning traffic helps to stop roads from becoming jammed and makes it easier to use for straight-on traffic.

**12.** You should stop. However, the green light will follow shortly, allowing you to drive on.

**13.** The GO signal on ordinary traffic lights consists of a single green light. The GO signal at automatic 'open' level crossings comes when the traffic light signals go out.

**14.** At Pelican pedestrian crossings.

**15.** The sign shows a set of red, amber and green traffic lights with a red bar diagonally across them.

**16.** No, wait until the road is clear. If you are kept waiting until the traffic lights turn red again, so be it!

**17.** a] Traffic would turn right or drive straight on.

b] Traffic would turn left.

c] Traffic would drive straight on.

**18.** No. This is the sign for No Through Road or Road Closed.

**19.** He is about to turn right.

**20.** No. Red and Amber together mean STOP.

**21.** Red and Amber.

**22.** If you are already across the STOP line when the amber light shows you may drive on, and you may also do so if, to stop, would mean an accident.

**23.** Red on its own. Red and amber together. Amber alone, except in the circumstances mentioned in the answer to Question 22, above.

**24.** There is only one, strictly speaking: the green light. Amber showing on its own can, in effect, mean GO but only in the circumstances mentioned in the answer to Question 22 above.

**25.** The double white line painted on the road at a junction means that you should stop there in order to give way to any traffic on the road running across. If the latter is clear, you may drive on. When a solid white line is painted in the same place, you *MUST* stop as a matter of course.

# A Driver's Tale (1) Answers

**1.** David saw the other car overtaking him out of his *LEFT* eye. This means he was being overtaken on the *LEFT*. Overtaking in such circumstances should always be on the *RIGHT*.

**2.** The driver *cut* in front of David after overtaking. The Highway Code specifically states that overtaking cars should not *cut* in front but should have enough room after overtaking to move safely and smoothly in front of the vehicle just overtaken.

**3.** No. David was driving at 40 mph on a wet road. He should therefore have reckoned 2 yards for every mile per hour of speed and the distance should have been 80 yards. Even on a dry road a 30 yard distance from the car in front when driving at 40 mph is too little. In these circumstances, the safe distance would be 40 yards minimum.

**4.** David should definitely *NOT* overtake, no matter what the provocation he has suffered. He should, instead, glance in his rear-view mirror to see that the gap between himself and any car that may be behind him is sufficiently safe for him to slacken speed and so drop back to a distance of at least 80 yards from the 'rogue' vehicle in front.

# A Driver's Tale (2)
# Answers

**1.** Unlike David, Anne and the children omitted to fasten their seat belts before moving off.

**2.** The red-edged, white triangular sign indicating Road Works and depicting a man with a shovel.

**3.** The zig zag lines were painted along the edges and the centre of the road.

**4.** The pedestrians were reluctant to cross because Anne gave the signal for a left turn, not the signal for stopping which she intended – this comprises moving the arm up and down.

# A Driver's Tale (3) Answers

**1.** David sounded the car horn at 11.27 p.m. The prohibition against sounding car horns in built-up areas begins at 11.30 p.m.

**2.** Yes. Three lamps going out reduced visibility in the road and must have increased the distance between lamps at that point to more than 50 yards.

**3.** Even though he was driving at night, when there would have been few pedestrians about, David kept to his daytime habit of looking to see if there were people crossing the side road he was about to enter. He did the correct thing.

**4.** Anne was sitting in the passenger seat which meant, of course, that 'her' side of the road was the left-hand, near-side. Allowing that the parked cars had the right to be parked where they were, all Anne had to do to notice incorrect parking was to count how many of the ten cars had their *fronts* to her as David was driving along. The four correctly parked cars were parked facing the direction of the traffic.

# Index